# Bull and the Red Saree

## Book for Change Makers

# RAHUL KUMAR

INDIA • SINGAPORE • MALAYSIA

# Notion Press

Old No. 38, New No. 6
McNichols Road, Chetpet
Chennai - 600 031

First Published by Notion Press 2020
Copyright © Rahul Kumar 2020
All Rights Reserved.

ISBN 978-1-64828-719-0

# Rahul Kumar

Rahul was born and brought up in Sasaram, a small town in Bihar. Later, he moved to Ireland and studied computer science and cloud computing with a scholarship from D.K.I.T. Ireland.

Rahul is the co-founder of an IT company "Revivo Technologies" that develops and innovates new technologies for Defence, media and other fields.

He was awarded and praised for the development of the mobile application "Saathi" by the Indian Army in 2015.

In college, Rahul had developed a platform named "Take-Stand" which achieved the milestone of over 1.5 lakh active users in just 2 weeks!

Rahul has also worked as a successful election strategist and has helped several popular political parties through his expertise in the field of technology and management.

Rahul has always taken a firm stand against social evils and has done a lot of social work through the Insaniyat Foundation.

His vision is to make our country a better place to live where there is no upper-lower and there is passion to fight for social justice and equality. The proceeds from this book will be donated towards women empowerment and social justice.

Email ID: hello@rahulnotes.in

facebook.com/irahul93

twitter.com/irahul93

Instagram.com/irahul93

# Foreword

Several issues that affect people the most in their lives have always been a matter of interest and concern for the author.

For example, we only care to dispose of the garbage polluting the environment in our homes, but when we see the same garbage polluting the road, we just cover our noses and walk past it, considering it not to be our 'personal' issue, to be the problem of 'society'!

The truth is that the issues that we usually choose to ignore, labelling them as social issues, are usually the problems which directly affect us.

This book raises questions on the discrimination and oppression against women. The very first chapter of this book, *Why just women?* raises questions on social evils like female feticide, the tradition of dowry, discrimination in the fields of education and occupation and domestic violence. It forces everyone to question whether these are the consequences a woman has to face just because she is of the female gender or because these evils have found their roots in the social order.

Regarding marital rape, this book emphasizes the fact that marriage in no way is a licence that permits one to enforce intimacy or violence in any manner.

This book has also highlighted the issues based on career and partner choices, where the book explains that if we do not make our choice regarding our career or life partner based on our parents' choices, then this doesn't mean that we are disrespecting them in any way.

If you are a change-lover and believe in empowering women and the youth, I'm sure you will love this book.

# Preface

First, I would like to thank you for selecting this book. This book has not been made as it looks. I have been sending you my reactions from time to time through such mediums as Facebook, Twitter and blog posts and this book is a result of only those articles and poems. I have always been interested in those subjects which affect our life more and more but which we label in our common language as social subjects and brush them aside. These are not social subjects but are personal subjects. We are getting into the habit of accepting whatever is happening in our society. We are ready to face unnecessary problems but are not at all prepared to finish their root cause. We have forgotten the saying "A small effort counts."

I have tried to write this book in such language that it can be easily understood even by an uncouth person when it reaches him.

This book has primarily been written with the youth being in focus because only the youth have that power which can build a better society. Today, our youth are carrying a treasure of information in their pockets; therefore, I have not written this book for the information of such youth. However, we still tend to look at problems as they are shown to us due to which we allow ourselves to believe that there is no solution to certain problems. Therefore, this book tries to show and look at some topics differently and logically. I hope you will find it interesting and useful.

# Contents

# After All, Why Only the Women?

I do not understand why parents do not kill their daughters in the womb itself if she has to lead a life of slow death if she has to suffer discrimination at every step. If she survives after birth, then she has to die due to dowry, and if she survives dowry, then she must die due to rape. If the killing of the girl foetus has to be stopped, then nothing will happen by merely raising the slogan of "Stop the killing of the female foetus!" because this is a contribution of circumstances. The attitude of society has to be changed. Even if we save girls at the time of birth, their individualities will be put in life-threatening situations at every turn.

To stop this, we have been demanding from the government, but we have not been doing anything significant at our individual levels. Perhaps there is no other country in the world where there is a law against gender tests before birth. The need arose for such a law in our country, which itself is a matter of great shame. How can the government stop this? For this, it will have to post a policeman in the bedrooms of all couples since this criminal act is planned by the couples jointly in the privacy of their homes.

If we really want to stop this, then we will also need to understand why people carry out such a dreadful act so easily. Why is there no killing of male foetuses? Why is it that only girls are killed before and after their birth?

When these questions arise in our consciousness, the answer presents itself automatically - dowry has to be given to the girl; the girl is the adornment of another family; the boy will render help in one's old age; the boy will take the ancestry forward and provide succession...

Out of these, the biggest reason is the problem of dowry. While families with resources can provide dowry, what about the poor? And if there is any delay in getting the daughters married off, then parents must face the sarcasm of the society - taunts that their daughter of marriageable age is living with her parents. I do not understand why the purpose of a girl's life is only to be married off and to serve their husbands and their families.

Due to the fear of dowry, the father destroys the girl before her birth itself; even if she survives, then her in-laws kill her over the greed of dowry. The custom of dowry is far more horrific than the erstwhile custom of Sati. Because in the custom of Sati, the wife was burnt alive only after the death of her husband, while in the custom of dowry, she is burnt alive when her husband is still living.

Now the question arises as to why people give or receive dowry. Its practice had started with the parents giving some money as a gift to their daughters at the time of their marriage. The father feels that she is our child, we have given birth to her, and so we should give her some gift.

So, the problem starts from here itself that we should give something. Why something? Why should the gift not be equal to what is given to the son? Is she not your offspring? Has her mother given birth to her in a different way? Is she not a human being? If the parents who gave birth to a child do not give her an equal right, then how can we expect someone else to give her the right of equal status and honour?

Since the amendment in Indian law which now gives an equal right of father's property to the girls, if a father does not give property to his daughter, then he is discriminating both socially and legally. Even today, the poor and lower-middle classes are not even able to provide proper education to their daughters because of the worry of arranging a dowry. She is not even given adequate education to be independent; she is only taught how to keep her husband and in-laws happy. When the parents themselves send their daughter to her in-laws as an amenity, then how can the others be expected to treat them as human beings?

Thus, in this way, having been deprived of education and property, girls become destined to remain dependent on their husbands for all their needs. From here starts the saga of the modern dowry system. If your daughter is a matriculate but if you are sufficiently rich, then you can get even an IAS officer as a son-in-law; getting a doctor/engineer is very common. The groom's family also accepts dowry with pride. The underlying thought is that a lot of hard work has gone into making the son highly educated and the woman marrying into the family will get all the comforts of life straight after marriage, so, money should have to be given in lieu of that.

Even while knowing that all these are wrong customs, those who have become IAS officers, doctors and engineers remain quiet, for if the person who is paying has no difficulty, then who dislikes money? I fail to understand that if you wish to have an educated girl, then why not make a search solely for the same? Why do you search for wealth from her parents? How can a girl be equated with money? This means that after marriage, you are not bringing a wife but a slave. Any girl is acceptable as long as her parents pay. If you think it over, then you will find your thoughts to be abhorrent.

The father of the girl also thinks that if his daughter goes to the family of a boy with a good status, then there should be no problem in giving some money. I ask you, which good home and what good boy? These people have no regard for your daughter, and they do not need a wife but a servant at home! How can you hope that your daughter will lead a happy life in such a house where she is valued even less than your money?

Remove the blinkers from your eyes and be aware that if you really want your daughter to be happy, then do not allow her to be dependent on fate and on someone else, but give her the strength and ability by which she can achieve everything on her own. If girls are provided education, made independent, are not differentiated against and given equal rights in house and property, then nobody will dare to demand dowry.

Some people talk about dowry, about the girls going to their in-laws and about the killing of female foetuses so normally, as if this was a natural rule or the will of God. It needs to be understood that this is our own creation, and this is a result of our mindset. Start the practice of getting your boys married and sending them to the girl's place. Provide education to the girls, teach the boys only how to keep their wife and in-laws happy, and give the property only to the girls and the freedom to earn money. Ask the boys to give up their house, name and life and to adopt the house, name and life of their wives. Then, it will be seen who is killed and who is tested for gender before birth and who gives dowry? It will also be known who is burnt alive for dowry.

There is a tendency to believe that girls are destined for this. If this is true, then do this once with the boys also and see the results. Friends, the problem is not with the gender, in being a boy or girl, nor in fate; the problem is with the social system, which is within the power of our parents. A father cares more and more for the opinions of society than the well-being of his daughter. He is taught to differentiate between his own children. As far as the question of becoming a source of support during old age is concerned, I have seen many girls who have nothing but go against their in-laws and serve their parents. So, if you give her equal affection and rights, then would she not be able to provide you with support during your old age?

If your daughter becomes self-dependent and is adequately rich, then nobody will show disrespect to her. Even then, if your son-in-law considers his wife a lowly being and does not give her due respect, then your daughter will not be helpless to live with him unhappily or to lead a life of suppression. She will have the economic freedom to leave. **In a happy situation, two people will live together for the reason that they love each other and not due to helplessness.**

This is also the reason for domestic violence. In today's world, women are still living with their in-laws despite being thrashed at home because of our social system. For this also, it is the parents who are responsible who provide neither education nor property and over and above do not lend support to their daughter. They tell her not to come back alive; otherwise, this will bring them a bad name. What kind of parents are these? Even animals do not abandon their children like this! For which society are you so worried, which has nothing to do with you or your daughter?

If you want that nothing wrong should happen to your daughter, that nobody should do injustice or differentiate with her, that your daughter lives a life of respect like your son, then it is you who will have to give it a start.

I also expect from the girls who are reading this article that they should not consider these problems as a matter of fate or to think that this is also because of their being females. They should make their parents understand and should fight for educating themselves and becoming independent.

# Violence Is Not Simply a Personal Matter

I had once gone to a relative's village. While the wooden cot was being arranged for me, the sound of someone's crying came from the neighbourhood. We ran in that direction and saw that one man was thrashing his wife like a wild animal. Perhaps there was some kind of discord between them. Some people were just standing and watching and a few were even laughing.

I rushed forward and grabbed hold of that man and pushed him aside. Then I asked the people who were present there, "Why are you laughing? Was he telling a joke while indulging in beating?" Those people responded by saying that this was the couple's personal matter, and no one else need interfere.

I was surprised as to how the people were treating the matter of violence as a personal issue. I asked them, "If tomorrow your brother or relative thrashes you and outsiders keep watching as spectators just because he is your brother or relative, then how would you feel?" They said that they would feel very bad. Whosoever may be causing violence, one gets hurt the same - whether you are thrashed by your brother or your enemy. Therefore, violence can never be a personal matter for anyone.

We have returned from there, but even today, whenever we read or hear similar news, we get a feeling of revisiting that place.

# Bull and the
Red Saree

Today, whenever there is an incident of rape, we as common people consider it our responsibility only to the extent of punishing the accused. Strong laws have been passed against rape, many of the accused have also got the death sentence, but the occurrences are not ending. The reason for this is that everyone in some way thinks that the incidence of rape happens because of someone's uncontrolled desire for sex. This is not at all due to this. If this was so, then why do only males do this? Do women not have such a desire? Therefore, it is totally wrong to say that this happens because of the uncontrolled desire for sex.

Someone can do such an act only when he becomes so self-indulgent that there is no feeling of remorse even if a person's life is ruined. He can do this only when he looks at a woman as an object or thing. When a person can kill for money, then he can also rape for sex. In other words, such occurrences will take place only where people are taught to think only about themselves and not to think about the extent of damage they cause to others. If we inculcate such teaching in our children, then in future, they will also work towards their selfish ends.

Many people feel that rapes happen because of the way of dressing. If you read the rapists' interviews, then it is known that the rapists also entertain such thoughts. However, what needs to be understood is that if this was so, then the women wearing full veils would not be victims of rape. How can an infant girl of two years be found to be alluring?

History shows that rape has also been used as a punishment for women. When she did not follow the social customs, then this was done to teach her a lesson. The male-dominated society treated this as a display of power and as a means to teach a lesson to the woman. Such men are those people who think that women should remain in restraint; they should behave only according to the social tenets made for them or as per tradition. They should not step outside during the night and should not have boyfriends or get into companionships with males. Rapists also hold such views.

*It is because of such views of some people that they are knowingly or unknowingly giving encouragement to rapists. In a way, they are giving encouragement* to the views of the oppression of women and advocating inequality. This mindset is also reflected in many religions, which have different rules for men and women. It is not correct for us to accept these blindly.

Such attitudes appeared to be clearly visible when the interview of the accused in the Nirbhaya incident in India was broadcasted. If you see that video, then it will be clearly understood about what kind of mentality and views those people had when they committed the crime.

To ensure that our children do not have such mentality, they will have to be taught about equality. Instead of teaching about certain tasks being meant for boys and the others for girls, parents should themselves give equal love, education and a share in property.

In addition to this, instead of treating girls as delicate and vulnerable, there is a need to make them strong and capable of defending themselves. Sex education should be made compulsory in schools and parents should make children understand this as soon as they reach puberty so that the child does not receive information on the subject of sex from objectionable sources.

Nowadays, the incidence of marital rape is very common. **It also needs to be questioned that marriage cannot be a licence to create a forcible physical relationship with someone.** For this reason, many girls who have not been able to gain independence and who are worried about the social stigma silently suffer these problems. Such girls need to be independent and they also need not at all worry about a society which is totally insensitive towards them.

The incidence of rape is an outcome of this unequal male-dominated society, which can be completely eradicated only by gender equality.

# We Live Only Once

Whenever there is a discussion about career, the first thought that comes to my mind is what Einstein had said about everyone being intelligent, but if you measure the ability of a fish with its capacity to climb the tree, then the fish will believe throughout life that she is foolish.

Today, there are more unsuccessful people than successful people and the biggest reason for this is that most people look at a career only as a means of making money. We often forget that money or success is not because of a particular field but because of one's ability in that field. In a field in which you think that there is a lesser scope for your progress but you enjoy working there, then the possibilities of your becoming successful are greater than other areas.

As soon as we complete our schooling, we start thinking about which career we should choose. Many boys and girls choose any career by regarding it as a source of mere livelihood, but they fail to understand that their work and career are the most important part of their life. They don't realize that this is where they are going to spend the largest chunk of their time.

Today's youth are also not being able to reach the peak of success because the objective of their life has been limited to themselves and to their life only. We forget that eating, drinking, sleeping and raising a family is also done by animals. If we are doing only the same, then what is the use of being born as the most intelligent living being on earth? As long as our life remains restricted to ourselves only, we cannot fix any bigger goal. In the same way, if a child has merely to pass his examinations, then he will never work hard to obtain good marks.

I often look at life as a situation where I have been left on some unknown planet, and it depends upon me as to how I should spend my time so that the opportunity of my having to come to this unknown planet is not wasted. The special thing about life is that it does not have a particular aim; this means that anybody can choose an objective of one's own choice.

There are two kinds of youngsters. One, who are told by their parents that they must do as their parents say - you have to take this path; this is your aim. They obey accordingly. Second, who question the purpose of these objectives and who themselves search for the objective of their life; they take their own decisions and walk the path of their choosing. Now, this is up to you to decide what kind of youngster you want to become.

Often, we question what should be the goal of our life or we ask as to what we should do with the time available. We try to understand what is important for us. The next question that arises is where we should invest the important time of our lives. The answer to this question can be found in different ways. I usually find the answer to this question by thinking that if this is the last year of my life then what would I do?

This book is also an outcome of that. I did not want to die without sharing my experiences. If you know what you find interesting and of your liking and by doing that you feel good, then you should do that; otherwise do not stop, but keep searching for that.

Many times, we know what we want, and yet we are not able to make efforts towards achieving that. In such a situation, motivational thoughts are helpful.

You should keep a copy of anything like some talk, a photo or video or anything which motivates you and you should also keep it in mind to regularly inspire yourselves.

In the same way that having a bath only on one day is not sufficient, similarly motivating oneself only for one day does not help much. According to a study by Harvard University, 85% of the success of a person is dependent upon one's attitude (way of perception and thinking). Opportunities are always available to us; we simply delay in recognizing them. It is always important to keep in mind that every problem brings an opportunity equal or greater than itself.

It is essential to create a positive atmosphere for that. A positive atmosphere works in the same way as the flow of a river. If you have to go in the direction of the flow of the river, then you will find it very easy; otherwise, if the flow is in the opposite direction of where you are going, then you will have to work twice as hard.

The definition of success is different for different people, but the method of success of everyone is the same. This can be easily known by knowing the common characteristics and collective qualities of successful people. There is another ailment which acts as a big obstacle in our paths, which we call in common language as to defer till tomorrow. **However, if we can do some work today, then it should be done today itself because we have very limited time available with us.**

We need to understand that if we lose most of our important time in sleeping, relaxing, eating and bathing, then when we will complete the important tasks of life?

We think that when we become adults then we will do this and that and then we go on postponing all tasks to the next day, next month and next year. We need to understand that we are growing older every day; in this way, we may never be able to fulfil our dream by the end of our life.

*Many people have more money than the number of days that are available to us in our life. They spend their money carefully but not their time. While the money saved will be of use for our children, but our time that we are spending aimlessly will not be of use to anyone. If the money goes to waste, it can be earned again, but lost time cannot be regained.*

Therefore, we should use more and more of our time either to find the purpose of our life or to achieve our goal. Otherwise, it will amount to coming and going in the same condition. Therefore, you will have to give meaning to your life.

# Hatred and Social Media

I have been thinking for a long time as to where so much hatred and anger comes from. Then I thought about getting information about today's news from Facebook and Twitter and reading the reactions of other people.

Suddenly, I started paying attention to my news feed and found that the algorithm of Facebook keeps us engrossed on Facebook for a longer time. For this purpose, Facebook starts giving us posts of the same type due to which our news feed gets filled with posts of a similar mentality. For this reason, while our one viewpoint gets stronger, we do not get the opportunity to know other viewpoints.

Often we get the posts of such pages or friends, who try to cause anger by deviating from logic. Many times, I notice that so much cruelty is shown about the society from which we come or about which we remain concerned - whether it is Hindu, Muslim, Dalit, Christian or Sikh - that we start seething with anger. Instead of being sympathetic, we develop animosity towards other religions. We are not able to notice when we change from being a protector of one religion to a destroyer of another religion.

We, the youth, start getting so enraged with a sense of revenge that we hardly notice we have stopped being good human beings. Sometimes we even get connected with those violent and fundamentalist outfits who, for the sake of religious madness, do not shirk from using children for violence. Then we start telling the youth that we have simply given a befitting reply to the atrocities the other religion has done. However, we forget that the reply has not been given to them but to thousands of innocent children, women and aged, who are not even remotely connected with these incidents.

Very often such incidents are the creation of political parties so that there may be animosity in the society and they may benefit from the vote bank of one group. Thus, so much hatred is created that we fail to notice the divisions developing within our country. We also forget that we can never help any society, country or humanity by spreading hatred.

Our country is inhabited by people of many languages, races, religions and cultures and it is probably for this reason that our country is unique. Any place having so many diversities will naturally have differences of opinion, but this does not mean that we should consider anyone as our enemy. I truly believe that any thought or opinion can be expressed without hurting the feelings of others.

# Being Bihari

Sometime back, I was searching for a flat to rent in Pune. Being from Bihar, I faced too many problems. I still do not know what went wrong with good flat owners on knowing me to be a Bihari. Such problems could be faced by people coming from other regions or states. However, the question arises how this image got spoiled and how to improve it?

Many leading doctors, engineers and high officials from Bihar make every effort to hide their identity. Supposing you consider yourselves to be a good person, your behaviour will also be good. But if a person like you conceals his identity, then how will the people outside know that there are many good people also in Bihar? A thief who is caught in Bihar, calls himself Bihari, but when an officer shies from calling himself Bihari, then how will the image change?

I have also faced problems on many occasions for being a Bihari, but the solution does not lie in hiding one's identity. How long can you hide? If you hail from a place which has a bad image, then you have twice the responsibility that when you go outside, you should keep in mind that you are not merely representing yourself, but you are representing a state.

# Baba, What Is the Religion About?

When I was young, some child asked me about which religion I belonged to. At that time, I could not understand anything and said that I would let them know tomorrow. On reaching home, I asked my Baba (grandfather), "What is this thing called religion? And what is our religion?" He said, "What is good to be adopted and followed, only that is religion." **Then I asked again, "What is good to be adopted?" He answered, "What is beneficial for humans, equality, unity and justice, that is good to be adopted.** That is our true religion."

*Then I asked about humanity, unity, equality and justice, one after the other. He answered that the conduct and behaviour which we find to be bad for us, that we should not do to others, that only is religion.*

For example, if someone tries to exploit us, then we will not find it to be good; therefore, we should also not exploit anyone and should also raise our voice against it. If someone ill-treats us, then we will find it bad; we should treat everyone as equals. Nobody likes injustice; therefore, we should support justice.

He again stated that if parents give birth to a child, then it becomes their religion that they should bring him/her up in the right way, give him/her lot of love and affection and good education so that the child may know and understand this world properly. It becomes the religion of the child that he should treat his parents with respect, give them love, be of service to them and when they grow old, he should give them the same love and affection that he got from his parents.

"It should be the religion of our teacher that he should always first motivate his disciple to be a good human being, then he should offer knowledge."

So I asked, "Is caste also a similar thing?" He said, "No, the different types of living beings are called castes, such as humans, lions, sheep, goat, elephant, dog, leopard, etc."

**"Then why do people ask us about our caste, aren't they able to see?"**

*He started smiling. He told me that people lack intelligence and take pride in showing themselves to be of a higher status, but such people do not possess anything to be of a higher status. Therefore, such people do all these false things, and many people get such things from their families for no cost and people do not think much about free things.*

Then I asked my grandfather if I must tell all this to my friends in class. He replied that I should merely say that I am a human being and my religion is humanity. If my friend asked, then I should tell him what this is about.

However, **I feel sorry that on growing up, I found that religion is different for this world. Here, people take pride in considering themselves more to be Hindus, Sikhs, Christians or Muslims than to be humans.** They also do not raise questions about their religion; they blindly follow what is written. They seem to be in a race to call their own religion to be greater. All this does not end here; they try to force others to follow their lifestyle and sometimes go to the extent of harming each other.

**I feel a deep sense of anguish on seeing that here religion does not exist for humans, but humans exist for religion.** I felt that if others' grandparents shared the thoughts of my grandfather, then the conditions would not be so bad. However, that is not possible; but there is one way, that all the children can learn these things through education. They can learn through the medium of education, and I hope that the children of our country receive such education at the earliest so that instead of taking pride in being Hindus, Sikh, Christians and Muslims, they take pride in being good humans.

# I Am Not That Bad - God

I think that many people are religious only because they feel that religion has been created by Bhagwan or Allah and God wrote religious inscriptions. The day they understand that God cannot state two different things, that too opposite to each other, that God cannot have so little knowledge to write in some place that the earth is like a saucer being balanced on a multi-headed cobra and at another place that it is like an egg, on that day the preaching places of religion will be shut down.

**I do not understand why people consider God to be so cruel or mad that he will punish in this birth for the sins of previous birth and even for that mistake about which he is unaware.**

How can He be anti-women? How can He state that the woman is an invaluable possession, meaning that she is an article to keep under control? That you can also indulge in beating her? How can He make different rules for women and men? A man may marry any number of times he wishes but a widowed woman does not have the right to marry even once? No, He cannot give step-motherly treatment to his children?

If He has done this, then I cannot worship Him only because he has given me life. For example, if a mother throws away a child to die after giving it birth, then that mother is not worthy of worship. In the same way, if you say that God is so bad and cruel, then I am against such a God.

Friends, God shows us the right path and does not indulge in worthless talk to mislead us. He has gifted us intellect to think so that we do not trust what others say but believe in something on the basis of logic and fact. If he needed to send ritualistic men, pundits, maulvis and priests to lead us on the right path, then we would not have been given intellect. Probably He would know that some people are also cunning and knowing that I will never appear, and the cunning may not take advantage of this; therefore, he gave us brains to think.

Even after studying history and science, why don't you understand when religion was introduced and for what purpose? If you are not aware, then you need to study history. Then the whole story will be clear.

The day all of you become aware that God did not create religion, on that day the places of preachers of religious falsehoods will disappear. The day you feel that God is omnipresent, on that day you will stop visiting temples, mosques and churches and will stop lavishing crores of rupees on those places and instead will give that money to society. The day you feel that our deeds are our worship, on that day, you will not spend long hours worshiping him. The day you realize that all our belongings have been given by God and that God does not crave for our offerings, on that day a new world will create shape where there will be equality, brotherhood, equality and a just system. You will be guided by your intellect about your religion, and you will not be guided by a self-styled guru but by your own conscience.

I am writing this article in the hope it will reach particularly those people who take greater pride in being a Hindu, Muslim or Christian than being a good human being.

# The Philosophy
# of Exploitation

On the day that victim died, my friend said something abnormal. He said that whatever happens is according to our fate; that this girl had this written in her destiny. He did not stop at this and again stated that she must have done something vicious in her previous life due to which this has happened to her.

People ask what *Brahmanvad* is. Fatefulness, rebirth, casteism, racism, religious shams, are all collectively called *Brahmnvad*. On the basis of these principles and views, women and lower castes were exploited, and they silently suffered thinking that this is written in their fate according to the deeds of the last birth.

I am against religious scriptures also because these things have been deeply ingrained in them. Those who have only heard about these should kindly read their religious scriptures for themselves.

I have complete belief that if you are a supporter of equality and freedom of humans, then you will turn more against these. You worship these only in those situations when either you are not aware of what is written in these or you get some kind of benefit from that particular religion.

There are some other people also who are trying to prove their religion as the best merely because they have already adopted it without thinking about it and have accepted it as correct. I do not say that God does not exist; I am saying that God cannot be so cruel or senseless that He will punish for the last birth for the mistakes about which we are not aware.

**Psychological slavery is also peculiar; the slave does not get to know that he is a slave.** Howsoever bad may be the condition of the last birth, he accepts it and continues to live by treating it as a fruitful result. In fact, in today's world, not to question is mental slavery, irrespective of who is saying or how many people are accepting that situation. Whether it is a question of choosing one's career or a partner, to blindly move with the herd is actually mental slavery in today's times. Not to talk about faith - belief and logic are done only by two kinds of persons, either imposters or fools.

# The Beauty of Life

The beauty of life is how you view it,
So what, if a few pages were torn,
So what, if a few pages led you to mourn,
So what, if a few pages could not be borne?

The charm of life is how you view it,

Don't get stuck in that sorrowful minute,
Don't reel out your precious moments in it,
Life goes on with memories in tow
You may find treasure in these pages, you never
know.

Flip through the book of life at least once,
A lot of sad pages were turned, now it's the time for
joyous ones.
You cannot enjoy its charm without a try,
Flip through the rest of the book for what is yet to
go by.

The beauty of life is how you view it,
There shall be such a morn, you never knew it.

The charm of life is such
That your outlook on it is always in a rush.

Life carries a soul within its lifeless pages,
Let your present mould it with consciousness.
Let not God write your book with benevolence,
Let your present mould it with consciousness.

A smile works wonders in hard times,
Even a little attempt at courage chimes.
Moving on will not reduce the pain,
But the feelings might bend.

If the words don't fit, come through it,
The beauty of life is how you view it.

# My Mighty Pen Says

My mighty pen says, "It's time to wake up,
It's time for the walls in humanity to blow up.
Rahul, show them the path of religion,
And shut down the religious prison.

Rahul, burn the scriptures turning men to their
fellows;
Enlighten about the fallacy of these scriptures'
echoes.
Equality isn't lost, folks,
Let the candles of morality eradicate the hoax.

Rahul, wipe out the discrimination with a shower of
hopes."
The mighty pen says, "Let your words be the air
they breathe,
Let your words, in their hearts, seethe,
Let them weave a story on those blank sheets,
Give them a reason to fight till they're at peace.

Rahul, no matter your presence or your pages'
They should not be able to let go of your traces."

# Taking the Scriptures with Them

Taking the scriptures with them,
They're onboard a journey marked with mayhem.
Carrying sinewy words on their tongue,
They've embarked on a quest that stung.

They speak of their religion greatly,
Yet, everyone suffers gravely.
You religious way of living
Cannot proclaim another's way of living.

By understanding God and his defensibility,
We need not fall into the fallacy of his safety.
Human is not for religion,
Religion is for human.

Our judgement gets uneven
Amidst the indifference between faith and reason.
According to you, the Lord has written about
gender discrimination,
Yet, you preach him, as per your own ideation.

Taking the scriptures with them,
They're onboard a journey marked with mayhem.
Carrying sinewy words on their tongue,
They've embarked on a quest that stung.

Using God as a weapon,
They preach for every crime as a past life's lesson.
These connoisseurs of the Lord,
Use fatalism as an exploitative sword.
Mothers, playing second fiddle
Birth these prideful bodies with an acquittal.

They call themselves saints
Of the religious estate.
Claiming to change our luck, these peddlers
Have come out as generous pretenders.

Women get cremated when alive,
either in the name of Sati or dowry –
Culture and tradition become wild cherry.

The religious rules have changed conveniently,
Exploiting caste and gender very easily.

Taking the scriptures with them,

They're onboard a journey marked with mayhem.

Carrying sinewy words on their tongue,

They've embarked on a quest that stung.

# You Never Spoke

You never spoke, when they questioned your birth,
You never spoke, when your right to study was hurt,

You never spoke, when your brothers played
and you became the domestic bird,
You never spoke, when the ornaments decided your
worth,

You never spoke, when you adorned your hands
and feet with shackles of jewellery,
You never spoke, when you were gazed at and
consumed unduly,

You never spoke, when your clothes were responsible
when they touched you crudely,
You never spoke, when for marriage you were
presented as an object of beauty,

You never spoke, when your ownership rights were
by your family,
You never spoke, when your whole identity changed
so casually,

You never spoke, when you were sealed as his,
having vermillion of 'his' name,
You never spoke, when for not having a child,
you were blamed,

You never spoke, when you were bound in four walls
and tamed,
You never spoke, when you wore a veil of dignity
and shame,

You never spoke,
when your goodbye to this world was a bit blurry,
You never spoke,

when you became a domestic slave in your own
love story,

You never spoke, when you were charred for dowry...

Is wrongs and crimes enough
Or your silence?

# Pluck the Flower
# You Love

How can you call it love when you tamper your
flower?
How can you call it love when you cage your bird in
a tower?
You put her under a veil
Not for love, but to curtail.
You destroyed the flower you were supposed to
love.

The flower also has a heart and breath,
Your love for her has become her myth.

Is this your love that makes her dead inside?
When this love of yours becomes her suicide?
How can you call it love when you tamper your
flower?
This wretchedness isn't called love,
But it is a yearning to acquire all the above.

The line blurs between acquire and love.
If only they would know how liberating love can be
You destroyed the flower you were supposed to
love.

# The Ashes of
# My Burnt Pages
# Will Rise

The ashes of my burnt pages will rise
Into the era where hearts will revolutionize.

Only when unaware, the oppressed
Will endure the exploiting protest.
There'll be no patrons of religion
When they'll see that it's just their own edition.

My engraved words
Will reside in the hearts of these birds,
You cannot enslave the unaware,
Who makes it their affair

To fight for everyone's welfare.
The radiance of discipline and curiosity
Will erase all of the religiosity.

Women when they'll know their power,
Will not be caged in a bell tower.

The breeze of love will
Bring the barriers of caste downhill.
My burnt pages will speak volumes
The ashes will sway away your bleeding sand
tombs.

# What's in My Heart

There's a small window in my heart,
A child is peeking through the part,

He sees the world better than you,
With his tiny eyes and everything anew.

Appalled, he's on a lookout,
To save this world from a fallout.

His young hands leading the way,
His tiny feet trotting through the hay,

Apprehensive of the hatred,
He knows his love is sacred.

There's a small window in my heart,
A child is peeking through the part.

www.ingramcontent.com/pod-product-compliance
Lightning Source LLC
Chambersburg PA
CBHW051214250726
48655CB00006B/2411